NIMITZ AIRCRAFT CARRIERS

BY DEREK ZOBEL

BELLWETHER MEDIA · MINNEAPOLIS, MN

TM

Are you ready to take it to the extreme?
Torque books thrust you into the action-packed
world of sports, vehicles, and adventure. These books
may include dirt, smoke, fire, and dangerous stunts.
WARNING: read at your own risk.

Library of Congress Cataloging-in-Publication Data

Zobel, Derek, 1983-
    Nimitz aircraft carriers / by Derek Zobel.
        p. cm. — (Torque: military machines)
    Includes bibliographical references and index.
    Summary: "Amazing photography and engaging information explain the technologies
and capabilities of the Nimitz Aircraft Carriers. Intended for students in grades 3 through
7"—Provided by publisher.
    ISBN-13: 978-1-60014-222-2 (hardcover : alk. paper)
    ISBN-10: 1-60014-222-2 (hardcover : alk. paper)
    1. Aircraft carriers—United States—Juvenile literature. 2. Nimitz (Ship : CVN-68)—Juvenile
literature. I. Title.

    V874.3.Z63 2008
    623.825'50973—dc22   2008019869

This edition first published in 2009 by Bellwether Media.

The photographs in this book are reproduced through the courtesy of the United States Department of
Defense.

Printed in the United States of America.

CONTENTS

NIMITZ AIRCRAFT CARRIERS IN ACTION

The crew aboard a Nimitz aircraft carrier scrambles as an alarm sounds. A group of enemy bombers is approaching the **fleet**.

A call goes to the **flight deck** of the Nimitz. Pilots race to their planes. Three F/A-18 Hornets take off from the Nimitz to **intercept** the four bombers.

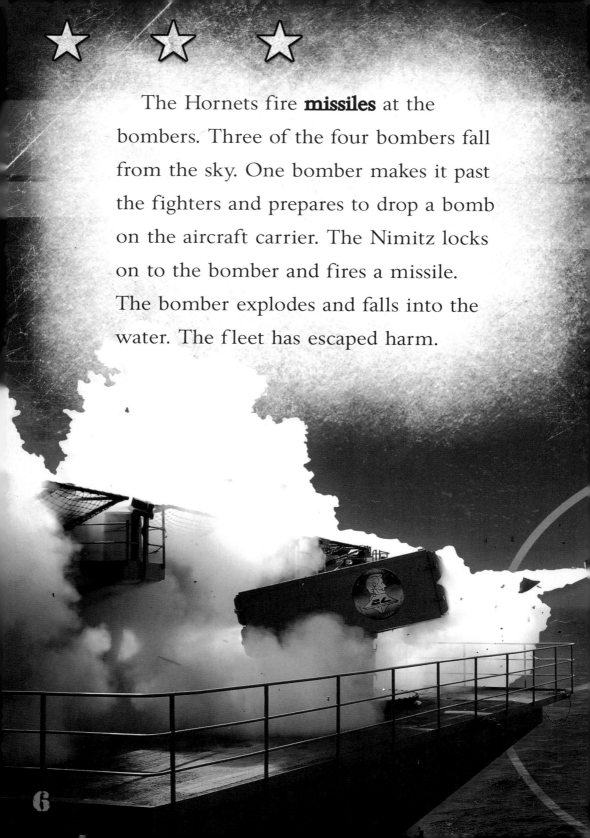

The Hornets fire **missiles** at the bombers. Three of the four bombers fall from the sky. One bomber makes it past the fighters and prepares to drop a bomb on the aircraft carrier. The Nimitz locks on to the bomber and fires a missile. The bomber explodes and falls into the water. The fleet has escaped harm.

Aircraft carriers were first used by the United States in World War II. They played a large role in defeating the Japanese Navy.

CAPITAL SHIP

Nimitz aircraft carriers are the **capital ships** of the United States Navy. The first Nimitz carrier was launched in 1972. Today, the Navy has ten of them. They are the heaviest warships in the world and have a crew of more than 6,000. They are powered by **nuclear energy**.

Nimitz aircraft carriers carry the
rcraft of the U.S. Navy and U.S. Marine
orps. The flight deck is 1,092 feet (332.9
eters) long. It has a runway on it for
rcraft to take off and land. There is also
om to park planes on the flight deck.
ther planes are stored below the flight
eck. Four lifts bring aircraft up to the
ight deck and down for storage.

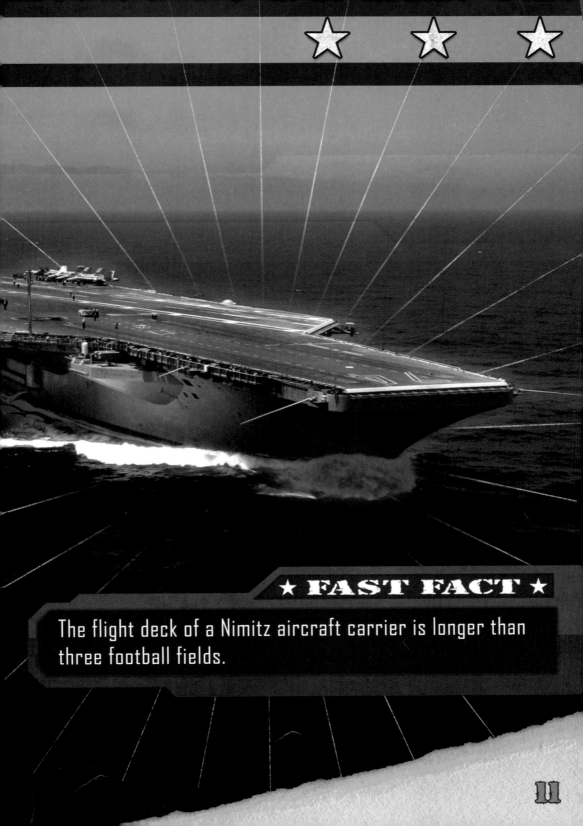

The flight deck of a Nimitz aircraft carrier is longer than three football fields.

WEAPONS AND FEATURES

Nimitz aircraft carriers carry many kinds of aircraft. F/A-18 Hornets are fighters that protect the fleet. EA-6B Prowlers fly ahead of the fleet and break up enemy communication. E-2 Hawkeyes gather information about the enemy. Seahawk helicopters perform search-and-rescue **missions** and protect the fleet.

★ FAST FACT ★

The wings and propellers of certain aircraft can fold up for storage below the flight deck of a Nimitz

13

Nimitz carriers also have weapons for protection. The RIM-7 Sea Sparrow is a surface-to-air missile that can shoot down enemy planes. The Phalanx CIWS can intercept missiles fired at Nimitz cruisers. RIM-116 Rolling Airframe Missiles can destroy targets in the sea, on land, and in the air.

16

NIMITZ SPECIFICATIONS:

Primary Function: Naval air support

Length: 1,092 feet (332.9 meters)

Width: 252 feet (78.6 meters)

Displacement: 97,000 tons
(87,996.9 metric tons)

Speed: 34.5+ miles (55.5+ kilometers)
per hour

Crew: 6,000+

Aircraft: 85

NIMITZ MISSIONS

Nimitz aircraft carriers are used for a variety of missions. During peacetime, their main mission is to patrol ocean waters. This helps keep the peace because few countries want to fight a capital ship of the U.S. Navy.

★ **FAST FACT** ★

Each Nimitz aircraft carrier costs $4.5 billion.

19

During wars, Nimitz aircraft carriers launch attacks at targets on land, in the sea, and in the air. They work with other ships and aircraft to defeat enemy forces. They also protect the fleet. Aircraft from Nimitz carriers can patrol the skies, perform search-and-rescue, and defend other ships. The many roles of the Nimitz make it important to the success of the Navy.

GLOSSARY

capital ship—a warship of the largest class; Nimitz carriers are the largest warships in the U.S. Navy.

fleet—a large group of ships

flight deck—the top deck of an aircraft carrier; aircraft take off from and land on the flight deck.

intercept—to prevent something, such as a plane or missile, from reaching its target

missile—an explosive launched at targets on the ground or in the air

mission—a military task

nuclear energy—the energy released during a nuclear reaction

TO LEARN MORE

AT THE LIBRARY
David, Jack. *United States Navy*. Minneapolis, Minn.: Bellwether, 2008.

Doeden, Matt. *Aircraft Carriers*. Minneapolis, Minn.: Lerner, 2005.

Green, Michael and Gladys. *Aircraft Carriers: The Nimitz Class*. Minneapolis, Minn.: Capstone, 2004.

ON THE WEB
Learning more about military machines is as easy as 1, 2, 3.

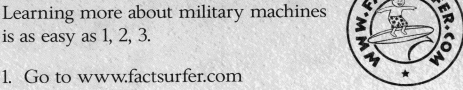

1. Go to www.factsurfer.com

2. Enter "military machines" into search box.

3. Click the "Surf" button and you will see a list of related web sites.

With factsurfer.com, finding more information is just a click away.

INDEX